T̲h̲e̲ Quail

retold by Bruno Bernardi
illustrated by Rex Barron

Harcourt

SCHOOL PUBLISHERS

Printed in China

ISBN 10: 0-15-350049-2
ISBN 13: 978-0-15-350049-7

Ordering Options
ISBN 10: 0-15-349938-9 (Grade 3 ELL Collection)
ISBN 13: 978-0-15-349938-8 (Grade 3 ELL Collection)
ISBN 10: 0-15-357259-0 (package of 5)
ISBN 13: 978-0-15-357259-3 (package of 5)

1 2 3 4 5 6 7 8 9 10 985 12 11 10 09 08 07 06

The Deer
and the

Harcourt

It was a sunny summer day. The animals of the forest were enjoying the perfect weather. Eagle was sitting on a tree branch.

Just then Deer came by. She was running gracefully through the woods. She moved like a dancer. Her fur was beautiful, as were her big brown eyes.

"It's lovely today, Deer," said Eagle.

"Yes, almost as lovely as I am," replied Deer. Deer thought she was the most beautiful animal in the forest. She smiled and showed her pretty teeth.

4

A moment later Eagle and Deer heard
a sound coming from a bush. They turned
their heads, and they saw Quail hopping
out of the bush. Quail was a small bird. Her
brown feathers had many spots on them.

Then Quail flew into the air. She went up
for a moment, and then she started to fall to
the ground. She flapped her wings as hard
as she could, and she finally reached the
branch where Eagle sat.

Deer began to laugh at Quail's performance. "Quail, you can barely fly, and your feathers are full of spots," said Deer. Quail looked at her spotted feathers.

"My spots may not be pretty, but they are helpful," said Quail.

"Oh, Quail, how could having all those spots on your feathers be helpful?" Deer asked. Then Deer leaped away, laughing at Quail.

Quail and Eagle looked at each other. "There are more important things in life than being pretty," Quail said.

The months went by, and Quail spent
her days looking for food. Sometimes
she saw dangerous predators, such as
foxes. Predators are animals that eat other
animals. Fortunately, Quail's spots helped
to camouflage her. She blended in with the
forest, so the predators did not see her.
Quail was safe.

Meanwhile Deer gave birth to a fawn. A fawn is a baby deer. Fawn had pretty brown fur and lovely eyes, just like her mother, Deer. Fawn and Deer took a walk through the forest one week after Fawn was born.

Deer and Fawn walked for a while until
Deer heard a noise behind them. She looked
back and saw a large bear coming closer.
Deer became frightened. She wanted to run
away. Of course she couldn't because she
had Fawn with her.

Just then Quail flew by. Deer called out
to Quail for help. Quail saw the bear in the
distance. Then Quail turned and flew over
to Deer and Fawn.

"You know how my spots blend in with
the forest? You have to blend in, too," said
Quail quickly.

Quail showed Deer and Fawn how to stand perfectly still as the bear approached. Quail put some sticks and leaves over them so that the bear wouldn't see them. Then Quail flew up to a branch. The bear walked right past Deer and Fawn without noticing them. Deer and Fawn were safe!

Deer was very grateful to Quail. "Quail, I am *so* sorry for making fun of you and your feathers," Deer said.

"I *told* you my spots were helpful," said Quail with a big smile.

Scaffolded Language Development

PRONOUNS Remind students that pronouns are words that can take the place of nouns. Model an example of changing a noun to a pronoun: _Deer was running. She was running._ Review the pronouns in the word bank. Then have students read the sentences below and chorally fill in each blank with a pronoun from the word bank that best completes the sentence.

Word Bank: her, they, she, it

1. Quail was upset. Deer was being mean to _____.
2. _____ said to Deer, "My spots help me because _____ keep predators from seeing me."
3. Deer laughed at _____.
4. Alone in the woods, Deer saw a mountain lion. Quail came to help protect _____ from the mountain lion.
5. _____ stood still together. The mountain lion left.
6. Finally, _____ were safe.

 **Social Studies**

State Symbols Tell students that the California Valley Quail is the state bird of California and that all states have symbols. Help students find out what some of the state symbols for your state are and make a list of them.

School-Home Connection

Talk About Helping Ask students to discuss this story with a family member. Invite them to have a discussion about ways that people can help one another.

Word Count: 513